THE MYSTERIES OF MATTHEW

An explanation of
The Kingdom of Heaven
The Sermon on the Mount
The Mysteries of the Kingdom

G. Michael Cocoris

Cover design by Victoria Marshal
Interior design by John Cocoris

TABLE OF CONTENTS

PREFACE

When I was in seminary, several of my classes covered the Gospel of Matthew. I was required to take courses in the Bible department that covered all 66 books of the Bible, including the Gospel of Matthew. The prophecy class needed in the theology department delved into the details of Matthew 13. In one or more of those classes, I was introduced to interpretations of the Gospel of Matthew that I found hard to accept.

For one thing, I was taught that there is a difference between the kingdom of heaven and the kingdom of God.

Another interpretation I was taught and did not accept was an explanation of the phrase "the mysteries of the kingdom" in Matthew 13. According to professors I deeply respected and who taught me a lot, the expression "mysteries of the kingdom" was a new form of the kingdom, a spiritual form of the kingdom, called Christendom. I did not understand how they got that meaning out of the text.

While I was in seminary, I did not resolve these issues. I was too busy studying to get through seminary and pastoring a church. I did not grapple with them until many years later.

When I became a pastor, I began preaching through books of the Bible one at a time. It became my desire to preach through every book of the Bible, but I deliberately put off preaching through the Gospel of Matthew because I didn't know how to solve my conflict with some of the interpretations I had been taught.

Finally, I was forced to preach through Matthew because it was one of the only books in the New Testament I had not covered. One of the books in my library on the Gospel of Matthew was written by Dr. Stan Toussaint. It was his doctoral dissertation. Dr. Toussaint had been one of my Greek professors and one of the best teachers I ever had. He was a godly man and a great teacher.

Dr. Toussaint's book solved my conflicts concerning the Gospel of Matthew. His interpretations made sense to me. In an email, I asked him how he came to his conclusions. He told me that when he was a student in seminary, Alva J. McClain, author of *The Greatness of the Kingdom,* delivered lectures in chapel that convinced him of the interpretation of Matthew that he adopted.

The purpose of this preface is to explain how I came to my views on the interpretation of the Gospel of Matthew. Simply put, I'm deeply indebted to Dr. Toussaint. As will be indicated in this book, I have accepted his interpretation of the kingdom of heaven and the kingdom of God as well as his explanation of "the mysteries of the kingdom."

G. Michael Cocoris
Santa Monica, CA

CHAPTER 1

PRELIMINARY ISSUES

Who wrote the Gospel of Matthew? To whom was it written? What is the subject, and how is that subject developed? What is the purpose of the Gospel of Matthew?

Author

The book does not identify its author, but early authors outside the Bible unanimously credit it to Matthew. For example, Papias (ca. AD 95-110; see Robert W. Yarborough, "The Date of Papias: A Reassessment," *JETS*, vol. 26, pp. 181-82) is quoted by Eusebius as saying Matthew composed the logia in Aramaic. If Matthew wrote in Aramaic, he later wrote in Greek. Josephus wrote *Wars of the Jews* in Aramaic and later in Greek. Only the Greek edition of Matthew has survived. Matthew was not conspicuous among the apostles, so it would be strange for tradition to assign the Gospel to him if he did not write it.

Critics claim that Matthew depended on Mark. They note that 92% of Mark appears in Matthew (606 of 661 verses). They speculate that Matthew is based on Mark and an unknown document they call "Q" (Q comes from the German word Quelle, meaning "source"). Matthew did not depend on Mark (and "Q"). He was an apostle; Mark was not. Why should an eyewitness depend on second-hand information? The writings of the early church fathers are clear that Matthew was the first Gospel to be written.

Recipients

The church was born and, at first, grew only in Jerusalem and Judea. Opposition soon developed (Acts 8:1-2). These circumstances suggest a need for a life of Christ, which would encourage persecuted Jewish believers and enable them to demonstrate that the gospel is not a contradiction of the Old Testament but a fulfillment. Matthew wrote to Jewish believers to demonstrate that Jesus was the Old Testament Messiah.

Matthew refers to Jerusalem as "the Holy City" as though it were still standing (Mt. 4:5; 27:53). He refers to Jewish customs continuing "to this day" (Mt. 27:8; 28:15). Therefore, Matthew was written before AD 70. Tradition says that after 15 years of preaching in Palestine, Matthew departed for foreign nations and left behind his Hebrew (Aramaic) Gospel. This would give a date of roughly AD 45 for the Aramaic Gospel of Matthew. Thus, Matthew was probably written from Syria, Antioch, or Palestine about AD 45-50. There are indications that these Jewish believers were undergoing persecution.

Message

The subject is Jesus Christ as Messiah, King of Israel. He is "the Son of David" (Mt. 1:1, 1:20; 9:27; 12:23; 15:22; 20:30-31; 21:9, 15; 22:45). The Magi seek the "King of the Jews" (Mt. 2:2). The prophecy of Micah 5:2 is applied to Him (Mt. 2:6). He is said to fulfill many prophecies and He is called the King (Mt. 21:5; 27:37). The message is Jesus is the Messiah who Israel rejected, died, rose, and commissioned His disciples to make disciples.

Structure

Five discourses dominate the book (60% of Matthew's 1,071 verses contain the spoken words of Christ): 1) The Sermon on the Mount (Mt. 5-7), 2) The Charge to the Twelve (Mt. 10), 3) The Parables of the Kingdom (Mt. 13), 4) The Teaching on Greatness and Forgiveness (Mt. 18), 5) The Olivet Discourse (Mt. 24-25). With slight variation, each of these discourses ends with the phrase, "Now it came to pass when Jesus had finished these sayings" (Mt 7:28; 11:1; 13:53; 19:1; 26:1). While not precisely the marker of the structure of the book, these discourses are a major part of this book. In the final analysis, the subjects covered in the book determine its structure. The book is not in chronological order.

Purpose

The first purpose of Matthew is to explain that, even though prophecies proved that Jesus was the Messiah/King, Israel rejected Him, so the kingdom was postponed and the church was inaugurated. Jewish believers faced a dilemma concerning Christ. The Jewish nation had expected a conquering prince who would establish a great Jewish kingdom. If Jesus were the Messiah, why was He rejected? What happened to the kingdom? How does the entity of the church fit into all of this? Was it the spiritual fulfillment of the Old Testament, or had God revoked the promises and covenants based on Israel's rejection? They needed clarification on Christ's relationship to the Old Testament, the kingdom, and His new-church purpose.

Matthew meets this need by repeatedly pointing out that Jesus fulfilled the Old Testament prophecies and promises concerning the Messiah. He uses more Old Testament quotes and allusions (about 130) than any other book to show that Jesus fulfills the qualifications for the Messiah. Matthew also deals with the kingdom issue. He refers to the kingdom of heaven 33 times, but the exact expression does not appear elsewhere in the New Testament. He first shows that when they rejected their king, the Jews rejected an earthly kingdom (Mt. 21:28-22:10; 11:16-24). Then, He shows that His kingdom is postponed. The promises of Israel are not canceled; they are yet to be fulfilled (Mt. 19:28;

20:20-23; 23-39; 24:29-31; 25:31-46).

In the meantime, God has inaugurated an entirely new and previously unknown program, the church. Matthew is the only Gospel in which the word "church" occurs. It appears three times (Mt. 16:18 and twice in 18:17). Because of the church's universal character, Matthew also emphasizes Gentiles. This can be seen in many ways: in his mentioning of two Gentile women in Christ's genealogy (Mt. 1:5), in his story of the wise men (Mt. 2:1-12), in his reproduction of the sayings that many from the East and West would sit down in the kingdom of heaven (Mt. 8:11-12), in his quoting the prophecy that Messiah would proclaim judgment to the Gentiles and that the Gentiles would hope in Him (Mt. 12:18-21), by use of the phrase "the field is the world" (Mt. 13:38), and by issuing the Great Commission to make disciples of all nations (Mt. 28:19).

The second purpose of Matthew is to encourage persecuted Jewish Christians in their faith. Christ was rejected. Hence, His followers will also be. In Matthew, there are no songs of joy at His birth like those recorded in Luke. His mother is almost repudiated and left in disgrace by Joseph. The Jewish male children are slaughtered. Jesus is only saved by a flight to Egypt. He is a despised Nazarene. He is rejected by the nation of Israel, His people. The account of the crucifixion does not contain a repentant thief or sympathy from anyone. His enemies revile Him. Even Matthew himself is a despised and rejected publican.

Summary: Matthew presents Jesus as the Christ, the King of Israel, who was rejected, who died and rose, and commissioned His disciples to make disciples among all nations.

If the Messiah, the King, is rejected, His servants will be too.

CHAPTER 2

THE KINGDOM

The Gospel of Matthew opens with John the Baptist preaching, "Repent, for the kingdom of heaven is at hand" (Mt. 3:1-2). Jesus preached the same message (Mt. 4:17). The Greek word translated "kingdom" means "royal rule, the territory ruled over by a king." In the Gospel of Matthew, the kingdom of Heaven is the royal rule of heaven, that is, the rule of God. What is the nature of the kingdom? Is it a spiritual kingdom in the hearts of people, or a literal kingdom on the earth?

A Spiritual Kingdom

Some argue that the kingdom is spiritual and present now. "He [John the Baptist] means 'the reign of God,' not the political or ecclesiastical organization which the Pharisees expected…. It is the fashion of some critics to deny to John any conception of the spiritual content of his words, a wholly gratuitous criticism" (A. T. Robinson). "The very demand of repentance, as previous to it, showed it was a spiritual kingdom" (John Wesley). "John meant that the dispensation in which, through the fulfilment of the Messianic prophecies …, heaven's (i.e., God's) reign in the hearts and lives of men would begin to assert itself far more powerfully than ever before, was about to begin; had even now arrived" (*Baker's New Testament commentary*). "With the arrival of Jesus in Galilee, the kingdom of God had become a present reality" (Tasker).

In the first place, this interpretation ignores the Old Testament concept of the coming kingdom and the first-century anticipation of that kingdom (see "an Earthly kingdom" below). Besides, God spiritually ruling in the heart was not near because the Old Testament recognized it was already here. The psalmist said, "The law of his God is in his heart" (Psa. 37:31). Furthermore, both John and Jesus said the kingdom they spoke about was "near," not "here."

An Earthly Kingdom

Several factors indicate that the kingdom of heaven is the literal kingdom on the earth that God promised to Israel. The Old Testament does not contain the expression "the kingdom of heaven," but it does promise a kingdom (2 Sam. 7:12), which is naturally understood as a literal kingdom. That is the way the Jews understood it. Daniel predicted that the Son of Man would destroy all the kingdoms of this world and establish an everlasting kingdom on the earth.

In the words of Daniel, "The God of heaven will set up a kingdom which shall never be destroyed" (Dan. 2:44). In other words, the God of heaven will set up a kingdom, the kingdom of heaven. In that context, it is natural to assume that since God would destroy literal, earthly kingdoms, He would set up a literal kingdom on the earth.

The prophets predicted a time of judgment followed by the Messianic age (Isa 4:4-6; Jer. 33:14-16; Dan. 7:25-27; Joel 3:12-18; Zeph. 3:8-14; Mal. 3:1-5; 4:1-6), which was understood to be a literal kingdom on the earth.

At the beginning of the first century, the Jews were expecting this Messianic Age, this kingdom, to be established on earth. In addition, the idea of some kind of a Messiah was "in the air" throughout the civilized world (McNeile on Mt. 3). The evidence for the expectation of a coming universal king is "abundant" (Plummer on Mt. 3). Barclay records some of the statements of ancient authors and adds, the "world was in eagerness of expectation" (Barclay on Mt. 3).

Since everyone at the time understood "kingdom" to be a reference to a literal kingdom on the earth, had John or Jesus meant something else, they would have had to explain what they meant by "kingdom," but they didn't, which means they meant it was a literal kingdom on the earth. So, when John the Baptist came preaching about the "kingdom of heaven," those who heard him knew exactly what he was saying. He was talking about the literal earthly kingdom God had promised the Jews in the Old Testament. The Kingdom of heaven is "the millennial kingdom" (Johnson, Jr., p. 35).

Summary: John the Baptist and Jesus preached that the literal, earthly kingdom promised in the Old Testament was near.

The kingdom of heaven was near, because the king was here. It was His work to bring the kingdom. McNeile states, "With the king is bounded up the kingdom." So, the kingdom was near because the king is here.

CHAPTER 3

THE KINGDOM OF HEAVEN

Matthew is the only biblical author who uses the expression "the kingdom of heaven" (33 times). The other New Testament authors who speak of the kingdom use the expression "kingdom of God." To complicate matters, Matthew uses the phrase "the kingdom of God" five times.

> **Matthew 6:33** "But <u>seek first</u> the kingdom of God and His righteousness, and all these things shall be added to you."
>
> **Matthew 12:28** "But if I cast out demons by the Spirit of God, surely the kingdom of God <u>has come</u> upon you."
>
> **Matthew 19:24** "And again I say to you, it is easier for a camel to go through the eye of a needle than for a rich man <u>to enter</u> the kingdom of God."
>
> **Matthew 21:31** "'Which of the two did the will of his father?' They said to Him, 'The first.' Jesus said to them, 'Assuredly, I say to you that tax collectors and harlots <u>enter</u> the kingdom of God before you.'"

Matthew 21:43 "Therefore I say to you, the kingdom of God will be <u>taken from you and given to</u> a nation bearing the fruits of it."

To sum up, Jesus said the kingdom of God had come upon them because He was present (Mt. 12:28). He speaks of entering the kingdom of God (Mt. 19:24; 21:31) and seeking it (Mt. 6:33). Because the Jews rejected Him, the kingdom will be taken from them and given to the Gentiles (Mt. 21:43). Is the kingdom of heaven and the kingdom of God two separate things or are they two names for the same thing?

Two Kingdoms Those who believe that the two are different argue that the kingdom of God includes only saved people (Jn. 3:3, 5), but the kingdom of heaven consists of both saved and unsaved people (the parable of the wheat and tares in Mt. 13:24-30, 36-43, especially the reference to those who practice lawlessness being "gathered out of His of kingdom" in verse 41). For this view, see https://walvoord.com/article/111#:~:text=Those%20who%20 distinguish%20the%20kingdom,enter%20the%20kingdom%20 of%20God.

One Kingdom Those who believe the two are the same point out that Matthew 19:23-24 uses both terms in consecutive verses to describe entering the kingdom, showing no distinction. Furthermore, Matthew uses "Kingdom of Heaven," where Mark and Luke use "Kingdom of God." What is called the kingdom of heaven in Matthew 5:3 is called the kingdom of God in Luke 6:20. Compare also Matthew 4:17 with Mark 1:15, Matthew 11:11 with Luke 7:28, Matthew 13:11 with Mark 4:11 and Luke 8:10, Matthew 13:31 with Mark 4:30-31, and Matthew 10:7 with Luke 9:2. How can these parallels be explained if the terms are not precisely the same in meaning?

But doesn't Jesus say that the lawless ones will be gathered "out of His kingdom" (Mt. 13:41), indicating that unbelievers are in the kingdom of heaven, which means that the kingdom of heaven, and the kingdom of God are two different things? A. T. Robinson, the famous 20th-century Greek scholar, said Jesus does not mean to say they are actually in the Kingdom of heaven. "They are simply mixed in the field with the wheat and God leaves them in the world till the separation comes." Robinson says see "from among the just" in verse 49. As Toussaint explains, "The judgment of the wheat and the tares occurs at the introduction of this kingdom; this judgment marks the beginning of His reign. Since this is so, it would be natural to say that angels will gather sinners out of His kingdom. Matthew 13:41 does not prove there is a present form of the kingdom consisting of believers and unbelievers" (Toussaint, "The Church and Israel," *Conservative Theological Journal* 2:7, 1998, p. 362).

Dillow agrees, "When Christ returns, the first order of business is to remove those who never enter the kingdom in a saving sense because they were not born again. Allen says, 'This must not be interpreted in such a way as to suggest that the kingdom is conceived of as a present condition of things within which tares and wheat grow together. When the Son of Man comes, then the kingdom also will have come. Hence, at that future date, the tares can be said to be gathered out of His kingdom'" (Dillow, p. 178; Allen wrote *A Critical and Exegetical Commentary on the Gospel of Matthew* in The International Critical Commentary series).

Why, then, did Jesus use both expressions "the kingdom of heaven" and "the kingdom of God?" Matthew, writing the Jews, uses the kingdom of heaven because the Jews use heaven rather than Yahweh out of their reverence for the name of Yahweh. Why then does He use "kingdom of God?" Toussaint says, "The kingdom of heaven denotes the fulfillment of the Old Testament prophecies, while the kingdom of God stresses the character of that kingdom. For instance, in Matthew 12:28, the character of God's kingdom is contrasted with that of Satan's. The kingdom of God is a more fitting term than the kingdom of the heavens.... Both terms always referred to the literal, earthly kingdom promised and prophesied in the Old Testament" (Toussaint, Kregel edition, p. 68).

Summary: The expressions "kingdom of heaven" and "the kingdom of God" are two different names for the same thing, the literal, earthly reign of Christ on the earth.

CHAPTER 4

THE SERMON ON THE MOUNT

Matthew records five major speeches of Jesus. The Sermon on the Mount is the largest. Beyond its place in the Gospel of Matthew, the Sermon on the Mount is, no doubt, the greatest sermon ever preached. To whom was it addressed? What is the subject and how is it to be interpreted?

The Audience

The Sermon on the Mount was preached to unbelievers and disciples. Matthew says, "And seeing the *multitudes,* He [Jesus] went up on a mountain, and when He was seated, His *disciples* came to Him" (Mt. 5:1, italics added). The contrast between the multitude and the disciples indicates that two distinct groups were present.

Undoubtedly, some in the multitude had not believed. The Sermon speaks of entering the kingdom (Mt. 5:20) and it ends with what sounds like an evangelistic appeal (Mt. 7:21-27). He taught the disciples (Mt. 5:1), but the multitude listened (Mt. 7:28).

The disciples were "His" disciples, meaning disciples in the strict sense (Plummer). Most of the Sermon is addressed to believers. Jesus says God is their Father (Mt. 5:16, 45, 48; 6:1, 4, 6, 8, 9, 14, 15, 18, 26, 32; 7:11). He speaks of future rewards (Mt. 5:12, 19, 46; 6:1-2, 4, 5, 6, 16, 18). The discourse concerns service and doing (Mt. 6:24; 7:24-27). It teaches the kind of righteousness a disciple should have in light of the coming kingdom. Thus, the content of the Sermon shows that it is addressed to those who had made some progress as followers of the Messiah (Alexander).

Thus, the audience consisted of believers and unbelievers.

The Subject

The subject of the Sermon is righteousness (Mt. 5:20). Real righteousness includes an internal attitude, not just an external act. See the summary of the Sermon below. It discusses rewards. The poor in spirit received the kingdom of heaven (Mt. 5:3). The meek inherit the earth (Mt. 5:5). Those persecuted for righteousness' sake received the kingdom of heaven (Mt. 5:10). Those who rejoice and are exceedingly glad when they are persecuted will be rewarded in heaven (Mt. 5:12). What is done in secret will be rewarded openly (Mt. 6:4, 6, 18). See also no reward (Mt. 5:46; 6:1, 2, 5, 16). Thus, the point of the sermon is how to live a righteous life to be rewarded in the kingdom.

Interpretations

The Sermon has been interpreted in many different ways. Biblical scholar Harvey K. McArthur identified 12 basic schools of thought, while another scholar, Craig S. Keener, found at least 36 different interpretations. These interpretations primarily grapple with the central question of how literally to apply the Sermon's high ethical standards to everyday life. Here is an explanation of some of the major interpretations.

1. **Double Standard View**. Widely accepted in the Middle Ages, this view divides the teachings into general "precepts" for all people and specific, higher "counsels" for a select few, such as clergy and those in monastic orders striving for perfection. This is the Roman Catholic view.

2. **Repentance View**. Martin Luther argued that the Sermon's impossible high demands are intended to make people aware of their sinfulness and their need for God's grace and salvation through faith in Christ, rather than as a set of rules for perfect living.

3. **Absolutist View**. This view interprets the Sermon literally, applying its teachings (such as pacifism and non-retaliation) directly to the lives of all believers in every age. God provides the Spirit to empower believers to obey these commands. This was the Anabaptist view.

4. Christian Living View. The Sermon describes Christian living. Jesus offered broad, general guidelines for behavior and internal attitudes rather than specific, rigid instructions. This is the Reformed view that applies the Sermon to the church.

5. Kingdom View. This approach holds that the Sermon's laws are primarily for a future "millennial kingdom" and were initially offered to the Jews, not the Church in the present age. Christians today can draw applications from its ethical principles, but are not strictly bound by all of its precepts. This is a traditional dispensational view.

6. Interim Ethic View. Associated with Albert Schweitzer, this view posits that Jesus believed the end of the world was imminent, and the Sermon provided an "interim ethic" for the brief period before the Kingdom of God would be established. Since the world did not end, these teachings do not apply to modern life.

Which interpretation is correct? Several factors must be taken into consideration to determine the accurate approach to the Sermon on the Mount.

First, at this point, the kingdom was being offered to Israel. Both John the Baptist (Mt. 3:1-2) and Jesus (Mt. 4:17) had preached, "Repent, for the kingdom of heaven is at hand!" The sermon itself indicates that the *coming kingdom* is a matter of concern. It speaks of entering the kingdom (Mt. 5:20; 7:21), being rewarded in the kingdom (Mt. 5:3, 10, 19), seeing the kingdom (Mt. 6:33), and praying for God's kingdom (Mt. 16:13) to come (Mt. 6:10).

Second, the subject of the Sermon is righteousness (Mt. 5:20). Genuine righteousness is not the external acts prescribed by the scribes and practiced by the Pharisees (Mt. 5:20). It is an internal attitude of love of God and others (see the overview of the Sermon below).

Third, the Sermon contains language that is not to be taken literally. For example, plucking out the eye (Mt. 5:19) and cutting off the hand (Mt. 5:30) are "highly figurative" (Plummer). Jesus is not teaching mutilation of the eyes or amputation of the hands. Jesus is using hyperbole. Even if a person plucked out his right eye and cut off his right hand, he would still have a left eye and a left hand. He uses absurdity to show that this sin is so serious that it requires severe action. No sacrifice was too great. Make no occasion for the flesh (Rom. 13:14). Cut off any people, places, books, magazines, TV channels, cell phone apps, or anything else that provides a temptation to sin. Anything that causes you to sin should be cut entirely out of your life.

Fourth, the interpretation of the Sermon must take into consideration spiritual truths taught elsewhere in Scripture. For example, in Matthew 5:22, Jesus said that calling a person a fool puts them in danger of hellfire, but in Matthew 7:26, He called someone foolish (the same Greek word that is used in Mt. 5:22).

Conclusion: The point of the Sermon on the Mount is that genuine righteousness will be rewarded in the future kingdom.

While Toussaint does not accept the theological position of Schweitzer, he concedes that a great deal of merit is seen in his approach to the Sermon.

Summary: The Sermon on the Mount teaches that genuine righteousness practiced during the interim between the comings of Christ and the kingdom will be rewarded in the kingdom.

AN OVERVIEW OF THE SERMON ON THE MOUNT

Introduction

    1. Real righteousness will be rewarded 5:1-13 (love God)

    2. Real righteousness will share 5:14-16 (love others)

    3. Real righteousness fulfills the law 5:17-20

I. Real righteousness has the right precepts 5:21-48

    1. Murder and anger 5:21-26 (love others)

    2. Adultery and lust 5:27-30

    3. Divorce and remarriage 5:31-32

    4 Oaths and speech 5:33-37

    5. Retaliation and love 5:38-42 (love others)

    6. Neighbors and enemies 5:43-48 (love your enemies)

II. Real righteousness has the right practices 6:1-18

    1. Giving 6:1-4 (as unto the Lord)

    2. Praying 6:5-15 (as unto the Lord)

    3. Fasting 6:16-18 (as unto the Lord)

III. Real righteousness has the right principles 6:19-7:11

    1. Do not lay up treasure on earth 6:19-24 (serve God, 6:24)

    2. Do not be anxious 6:25-34 (trust God, 6:30)

    3. Do not Judge 7:1-6 (minister to others)

    4. Pray 7:7-11 (depend on the Lord)

Conclusion: Love fulfills the Law 7:12

    1. Enter 7:13-14

    2. Beware 7:15-23

    3. Hear and do 7:24-27

A SUMMARY OF THE SERMON ON THE MOUNT

Matthew 5:3-12 God will bless now and reward later those who have internal righteousness.

Matthew 5:13-16 Believers are not to conceal spiritual truth from a decaying and dark world but to communicate it so that God may be glorified.

Matthew 5:17-20 Since Jesus fulfilled the Law, He can provide the righteousness necessary to enter the Kingdom and reward personal, loving obedience. To enter the kingdom, you must have faith. To be rewarded, you must obey.

Matthew 5:21-26 Since God and man will judge murder, anger, contempt, and verbal abuse, be reconciled with others as quickly as possible. For spiritual and practical reasons, settle controversies immediately.

The point Jesus is making is that not only the murderer is in danger of judgment, but also the one who is angry without a cause. The way He states all of this is striking. Notice, "whoever murders will be *in danger of the judgment*" (5:21, italics added), and "whoever is angry with his brother without a cause shall be *in danger of the judgment*" (5:22, italics added). By repeating the phrase "in danger of the judgment," Jesus puts anger without a cause on the same level as murder. Both are in danger of punishment. It was not just the act of murder that put a person in danger of judgment, but the attitude of anger, more specifically, being angry *without a cause* toward a brother. Jesus is not condemning all anger.

He got angry (Mk. 3:5). Paul said, "Be angry and sin not" (Eph. 4:26). Jesus is denouncing anger without a cause.

Matthew 5:27-32 Before God, adultery is not just the act but also intentionally coveting sex with someone to whom you are not married, and, except for sexual immorality, remarriage after a divorce is forbidden.

The point Jesus is making in this Sermon is that a correct view of righteousness is greater than the prevailing view of His day. The Jewish teachers reduced righteousness to mere external conformity to the Law. Jesus is teaching that it is the attitude of the heart as well as the external act that determines real righteousness. In His third example, He also says that even some external acts, such as divorce, are not in conformity with God's standard of righteousness.

Matthew 5:33-37 True righteousness does not need external guarantees of truthfulness, such as an oath; it is being truthful.

The scribes and Pharisees were concerned with "right" behavior. They thought that by right actions, they were right before God. Rule-keeping never makes one righteous. Jesus is teaching that real righteousness begins with an attitude. The issue is not that you have to do better. It is that you have to *be* better. Righteousness is not outward conformity to rules but "an inner response of a heart that is merciful and pure and seeks to make peace." The issue is not murder; it is anger. The issue is not adultery; it is lust. The issue is not divorce; it is selfishness. The issue is not the oath; it is deception (Robinson).

Moses says, "Do not lie under oath." Jesus says, "Don't lie under any circumstances." So, decide to tell the truth, the whole truth, and nothing but the truth when under oath and when you speak outside an oath.

Matthew 5:38-42 The righteous way to respond to insults, lawsuits, and impositions is not by demanding our rights or retaliating, but by giving up our rights and being generous.

This is not to say that you will not feel like retaliating. It is to say that when you have to decide what to do, you will choose to give up your rights, let the Lord handle the wrong, and be generous.

Nor is it to say that you should never demand your rights. Jesus Himself objected to unjust legal proceedings (Jn. 12:22-23). When falsely accused, Paul pleaded his legal rights as a Roman citizen (Acts 23:2-3). So what does this mean?

This was given to the disciples of Jesus (5:1). The issue is, "Do you want to be a disciple, a learner of Christ who becomes like Him?" Do you hunger and thirst after righteousness? Do you want to be meek and merciful from a pure heart that seeks peace? The real righteousness is not about rule-keeping but about relationships.

Matthew 5:43-38 Don't hate your enemies; love them by choosing to do what is best for them and, thus, become like God and be rewarded by God.

Matthew 6:1-4 If you give to the poor to be seen by others, you have your full and final reward, but if you give to the poor secretly, God will reward you openly.

Matthew 6:5-15 If you pray to be seen by others, you have your full and final reward, but if you pray properly in secret, God will reward you openly. Don't pray with empty repetitions to be seen by people; instead, pray with a forgiving attitude for God's will and for Him to meet your need for provision, pardon, and protection.

Matthew 6:16-18 If you fast to be seen by people, you have your full and final reward, but if you fast secretly, God will reward you openly.

The point Jesus is making in the Sermon on the Mount concerns real righteousness. He uses giving, prayer, and fasting as illustrations. Throughout these illustrations, Jesus repeatedly said that these things should be done in secret (6:4, 6, 18). In other words, real righteousness is an inward attitude of doing things as unto the Father in heaven and not to be seen by people on earth.

Another refrain that echoes through these illustrations is, "Don't be a hypocrite" (6.2, 5, 16). Hypocrisy will stunt your spiritual growth. Peter says, "Therefore, laying aside all malice, all deceit, hypocrisy, envy, and all evil speaking, as newborn babes, desire the pure milk of the word, that you may grow thereby if indeed you have tasted that the Lord *is* gracious" (1 Pet. 2:1-3).

Matthew 6:19-24 Believers should lay up treasure in heaven not only because material wealth is temporary and eternal treasure is permanent, but because it gives life true direction, which is undivided love and loyalty to the Lord.

Matthew 6:25-34 Do not worry about your material needs because if you trust God and seek His righteousness and will, He will supply your physical needs.

Matthew 7:1-6 Do not have a spirit of condemnation; rather, judge yourself so you can help others. Instead of pointing a fault-finding finger, hold out a helping hand. A spirit of criticism and condemnation is a form of self-righteousness, not true righteousness. We put others down to make ourselves look good.

Matthew 7:7-11 As a loving heavenly Father, God responds to the perseverance in prayer of His children when they ask for the good things that are according to His will.

Matthew 7:12 The Golden Rule is not just "do no harm"; it is "do good," which fulfills the Old and New Testaments.

Matthew 7:13-14 Although many do it, do not enter the gate or follow the way that leads to destruction; instead, enter the gate and follow the way that leads to life.

Matthew 7:15-23 Beware of false prophets who look like true prophets, speak like true prophets, and even do things true prophets do. The litmus test of a true prophet is whether or not he accurately conveys God's message as determined by God's Word.

Matthew 7:24-29 Those who build their life on the teachings of Christ weather the storms of life, but those who do not fall.

CHAPTER 5

THE PARABLES OF MATTHEW 13

After Jesus was rejected in Matthew 12, He began speaking in parables. He told the disciples that they were blessed because they were hearing things that the prophets and righteous men of old desired to see and hear but did not (Mt. 13:17). He told them that they had the privilege of knowing "the mysteries of the kingdom of heaven" (Mt. 13:11).

The problem is the meaning of the word "mysteries." The Greek word translated "mysteries" means the "counsels of God … once hidden but now revealed in the gospel or some fact thereof" (A-S; Mt. 13:17, 35). So, in Matthew 13, when Jesus speaks of the mysteries of the kingdom, He is instructing the disciples about the hitherto unrevealed information concerning the kingdom.

What is the new information Jesus is now revealing in the parables of Matthew 13? A view held by the ultradispensationalists is that the Sermon is for the Jews only. Other than that, there are three basic interpretations of the parables of Matthew 13.

To Correct their Concept of the kingdom

This view says that "the mysteries of the kingdom of heaven" means Jesus is correcting their concept of the kingdom. They thought the kingdom would be literal. Jesus is teaching that He did not come to establish an earthly kingdom but a spiritual one.

For example, Alexander says the mystery is "that of the kingdom of God, to be erected by Messiah in the heart of man and of society, and to receive its final consummation in a future state of glory." Did not Jesus say, "For indeed, the kingdom of God is within you" (Lk. 17:21 NKJV)? Many of this point of view equate the kingdom with the church (Alexander). According to this view, there is no literal kingdom on the earth.

This explanation completely disregards the Old Testament prophecies. Moreover, in this passage, Jesus said that the disciples were blessed because they did understand (13:16), and at the end of Jesus' life, they had the same idea of an earthly Messianic kingdom (Lk. 24:21; Acts 1:6). By the way, when Jesus said, "The kingdom of God is within you" He was talking to the Pharisees (Lk. 17:20) and what He said was "The kingdom of God is in the midst of you" (ESV).

To Introduce a New Form of the kingdom

A second interpretation of "the mysteries of the kingdom of heaven" is that Jesus is giving a *new form* of the kingdom, namely,

Christendom (Scofield; Chafer; Walvoord; Pentecost; Ryrie; Gaebelein; Barnhouse; Kelly; English; Feinberg; Pettingill). There will be an earthly Messianic kingdom in the future, as revealed in the Old Testament, but before it arrives, there is a *spiritual form* of the kingdom that is not the church because it includes both believers and unbelievers. Jesus said, "The Son of Man will send out His angels, and they will gather out of His kingdom all things that offend and those who practice lawlessness, and cast them into the furnace of fire. There will be weeping and gnashing of teeth. Then the righteous will shine forth as the sun in the kingdom of their father" (Mt. 13:41-43).

There are problems with this position. For one thing, the expression "the mysteries of the kingdom" does not mean a *new form* of the kingdom. The content of the parables indicates that the mysteries of the kingdom are the unrevealed truth about the kingdom (Toussaint). Also, this view says that the mystery form consists of both believers and unbelievers, but the kingdom of heaven is composed of believers (Jn. 3:5, 5, 7). For an explanation of Matthew 13:41-43 see pages 15-16.

To Reveal New Truths Concerning the Kingdom

A third explanation is that the kingdom of heaven in Matthew 13 is the earthly Messianic kingdom, and the mystery is the timetable.

"The truths relate to the time of the establishment of the kingdom, the preparation for it, and other material which had never been revealed" (Toussaint, Kregel edition, p. 175). Toussaint also says, "The parables of Matthew 13 reveal new truth involving the preparation for the establishment of the kingdom during the time of postponement, which was not predicted in Daniel's 70 weeks or other Old Testament prophecies." He argues that this view agrees with the Old Testament prophecies of the kingdom and is consistent with the New Testament concept of mystery. Commenting on Matthew 16:19, Plummer says, "In this gospel, kingdom seems always to mean that which the Son of Man is to begin at the Second Advent, which is regarded as near."

The kingdom is in the future. Later, in the Gospel of Matthew, Jesus taught His disciples to pray, "Your kingdom *come*" (Mt. 6:10, italics added). He said, "Blessed are the meek, for they *shall* inherit the earth" (Mt. 5:5, italics added). Within days of the crucifixion, when the disciples were seeking a position in the kingdom (Mt. 20:17-28), the Lord did not dispute their concept of the kingdom. At the end of His life, He said, "But I say to you, I will not drink of this fruit of the vine from now on until that day when I drink it new with you in My Father's kingdom" (Mt. 26:29). Commenting on Matthew 16:19, Plummer says, "In this gospel, kingdom seems always to mean that which the Son of Man is to begin at the Second Advent, which is regarded as near" (Plummer, p. 230) and "The Kingdom of Heaven is the kingdom, "which the Son of Man will come in the heavens to inaugurate" (Plummer, p. 177 fn.).

The proof that the kingdom John and Jesus preached is the future earthly kingdom is found in Acts 1:3-8. The disciples asked Jesus if He was going to "at this time restore the kingdom to Israel?" (Acts 1:6). There is no doubt that they were still expecting Christ to set up a kingdom, a literal kingdom on the earth, not a spiritual kingdom in their hearts. Nor were they mistaken. That is obvious for three reasons: 1) They had listened to Jesus teach about the kingdom for three years. 2) They had just heard Him speak about the kingdom again during the forty days since His resurrection (Acts 1:3). 3) Jesus did not correct them; He confirmed that what they were thinking about the kingdom was correct; it was just that they did not understand that this was not the time (Acts 1:7).

So, in Matthew 13, when Jesus speaks of the mystery of the kingdom, "He is instructing His disciples regarding the hitherto unrevealed period of time before the establishment of the kingdom. This new age would not be the promised kingdom, nor would it be, strictly speaking, a kingdom in the so-called 'mystery form.' Thus, the mysteries of the kingdom of heaven relate to a span in which the millennial kingdom is being postponed" (Toussaint, Kregel edition, pp. 171-172).

Summary: The Parables of Matthew 13 are not some "mystery form" of the kingdom, but reveal information concerning the time before the kingdom will be established.

A Summary of the Parables of Matthew 13

Parable of the Sower	Response is the result of the heart.
Parable of Wheat and Tares	Believers and unbelievers will co-exist.
Parable of the Mustard Seed	The growth of believers will be great.
Parable of the Leaven	The growth of unbelievers will be great.
Parable of the Tares	At the end, there will be a judgment.
Parable of the Treasure	Jesus gives all to gain believers.
Parable of the Pearls	Jesus gives all to purchase us.
Parable of the Dragnet	At the end, there will be a judgment.

CHAPTER 6

CONCLUSION

The Gospel of Matthew begins by indicating that the literal kingdom promised in the Old Testament was near and, in the Sermon on the Mount, Jesus taught His disciples how to be rewarded in the kingdom, but when He, and therefore, the kingdom was rejected, He explained that the kingdom would be postponed.

Here is a summary that explains how to interpret the Gospel of Matthew.

1. God made a covenant with Abraham to give his descendants the land (Gen. 15:5-7, 18-19).

2. God promised David that his descendants would have a kingdom in the land (2 Sam. 7:12).

3. Daniel 2 says, "The God of heaven will set up a kingdom which shall never be destroyed (Dan. 2:44).

4. John the Baptist preached, "Repent, for the kingdom of heaven is at hand" (Mt. 3:1-2). The kingdom is about to come.

5. Jesus preached, "Repent, for the kingdom of heaven is at hand" (Mt. 4:17). The kingdom is about to come.

6. Jesus taught that those who live a righteous life (Mt. 5:20) will be rewarded (Mt. 5:11-12) in the kingdom (Mt. 5:3, 10).

7. The Pharisees rejected Jesus (Mt. 12:14, 24), thus rejecting the kingdom of heaven.

8. What happened! In the parable of the Sower (Mt. 13:3-9, 18-23), Jesus explains that the problem is not the Sower (Jesus, the messenger), nor the seed (the message), but the ground on which the seed fell (the hearers).

9. Where do we go from here? Using parables [the wheat and the tares (Mt. 13:24-30), the mustard seed (Mt. 13:31-32), leaven (Mt. 13:33), and tares (Mt. 13:36-43)], Jesus explains that He is not going to establish the kingdom now. The kingdom will be postponed. During the interim, He will sow sons of the kingdom, and Satan will sow sons of the wicked one. Good and evil will exist until the end of the age, when God will separate the sons of the kingdom from the sons of darkness, and the wicked will suffer, and the righteous will shine.

10. The parables of the treasure hidden in a field (Mt. 13:44), the pearl of great price (Mt. 13:45-46), and the dragnet (Mt. 13:47-51), teach He will give all to gain believers and at the end, there will be a judgment, but in the meantime, those who understand the truth of the kingdom are to teach others.

At the end of Matthew 13, Jesus asked, "'Have you understood all these things?' They said to Him, 'Yes, Lord.' Then He said to them, 'Therefore every scribe instructed concerning the kingdom of heaven is like a householder who brings out of his treasure things new and old'" (Mt. 13:51-52). A scribe was a "professional expounder of the Scripture" (Alexander). Jesus is saying that if you understand all that He taught in this chapter, you are now like a professional expounder who has been instructed. You now have new and old spiritual treasures.

The point is now that they have been taught, they are to teach. Those who have been instructed are to instruct and those who have been told are to tell.

Bibliography

Abbott-Smith, G. *A Manuel Greek Lexicon of the New Testament*. Edinburgh: T & T Clark, 1960 (reprint of the 1937 edition).

Alexander, Joseph Addison. *The Gospel According to Matthew*. Lynchburg, VA: James Family Christian Publishers, ND (initially published in 1861).

Baker's New Testament commentary. e-sword.net.

Barclay, William. *The Gospel of Matthew*, 2 vol. Philadelphia: The Westminster Press, 1958.

McArthur, Harvey K. *Understanding the Sermon on the Mount*. New York: Harper and Brothers Publishers, 1960

McNeile, Alan Hugh. *The Gospel According to Matthew*. London: MacMillan & Co. LTD, 1961 (originally published in 1915).

Plummer, Alfred. *An Exegetical Commentary of The Gospel According to S. Matthew*. Minneapolis: James Family Christian Publishers, ND.

Robertson, A. T. *Word Pictures in the New Testament.* e-sword.net.

Tasker, R. V. G. *Matthew,* The Tyndale New Testament Commentaries. Grand Rapids: William B. Eerdmans Publishing Company, 1961.

The NKJV Study Bible. Earl D. Radmacher, ed. Nashville: Thomas Nelson, Inc. 1997

Toussaint, Stanley D. *Behold the King*. Grand Rapids, Michigan: Kregel Publications, 1980.

Wesley, John. *John Wesley's Notes on the Bible.* e-sword.net.

Yarborough, Robert W. "The Date of Papias: A Reassessment." *Journal of the Evangelical Theological Society*, vol. 26, 1983

About The Author

G. Michael Cocoris is a gifted communicator. He can make even complicated subjects simple, clear, and practical. His breadth of experience has allowed him to relate to a wide range of audiences.

Michael received a Bachelor of Arts degree from Tennessee Temple University, a Master of Theology degree from Dallas Seminary, and a Doctorate of Divinity from Biola University. He traveled the United States for over a dozen years as a speaker. He has also been a seminary professor, visiting lecturer, and world traveler, including hosting tours to Israel and China.

Michael has pastored three churches, including a rural church when he was in seminary, an urban church, the historic Church of the Open Door, first in downtown Los Angeles and later in Glendora, California, and a suburban church, the Lindley Church in Tarzana California, a suburb of Los Angeles. While at the Church of Open Door, he had a daily radio broadcast.

Michael has written numerous magazine articles, mainly for *Biblical Research Monthly*. He has authored a number of books, including *Seventy Years on Hope Street, A History of the Church of the Open Door; How To Live A Biblical Spiritual Life, Clarifying the Confusion; Repentance, The Most Misunderstood Word in the Bible; Evangelism: A Biblical Approach; The Salvation Controversy; Lordship Salvation: Is It Biblical?; The Books of the Bible, the Subject, Structure, Situation, and Significant Verses of Each Book; Psalms, A Song for Every Situation, Each Summarized on One Page; and Counseling Theories, A Biblical Evaluation.* In addition, he was a contributor to The *NKJV Study Bible* and *Nelson's New Illustrated Bible Commentary*.

Michael is the pastor of the Lindley Church in Tarzana, California. He and his wife, Patricia, live in Santa Monica, California.